BIG BOOK OF

UKRAINIAN

ALPHABET

FOR KIDS

CHATTY PARROT

Акула
Shark [akúla]

Автобус
Bus [avtóbus]

Акваріум
Aquarium [akvár'ium]

Аа

Ананас
Pineapple [ananás]

Авокадо
Avocado [avokádo]

Білка

Squirrel [b'ílka]

Бутерброт

Sandwich [buterbród]

Банка

Jar [bánka]

Бб

Будинок

Building [budýnok]

Букет

Bouquet [bukét]

Велосипед

Bike [velosypéd]

Веселка

Rainbow [vesélka]

Вікно

Window [v'iknó]

Вв

Вишня

Cherry [výshn'a]

Вовк

Wolf [vovk]

Гарбуз

Pumpkin [harbúz]

Гілка

Branch [h'ílka]

Гриб

Mushroom [hryb]

Г г

Гора

Mountain [horá]

Годинник

Clock [hodýnnyk]

Гава

Crow
[gáva]

Ганок

Porch [gánok]

Гг

Гудзик

Button [gúdzyk]

Газон

Lawn [gazón]

Дельфін

Dolphin
[del'fín]

Дзеркало

Mirror
[dzérkalo]

Дерево

Tree
[dérevo]

Дд

Диван

Sofa
[dyván]

Драбина

Ladder
[drabýna]

Еклер

Eclair [eklér]

Єдиноріг

Unicorn [jedynor'íh]

Ескімо

Ee Єє

Popsicle [esk'imó]

Єнот

Raccoon [jenót]

Жаба

Frog [zhába]

Жирафа

Giraffe [zhyráfa]

Жж

Жилет

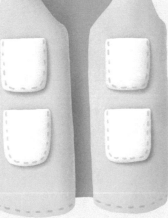

Vest [zhylét]

Жолудь

Acorn [zhólud']

Заєць

Hare
[zájets']

Зима

Winter [zymá]

Зз

Земля

Earth [zeml'á]

Зірка

Star
[z'írka]

Зебра

Zebra
[zébra]

Сир

Cheese [syr]

Виделка

Fork [vydélka]

Лис

Fox [lys]

Ии

Кит

Whale [kyt]

Килим

Carpet [kýlym]

Іграшка

Toy
[íhrashka]

Ії Її

Їжак

Hedgehog
[jizhák]

Індик

Turkey
[indýk]

Їжа

Food
[jízha]

Йогурт

Чайник

Йй

Kettle
[chájnyk]

Yogurt
[jóhurt]

Йога

Чай

Yoga   [jóha]

Tea   [chaj]

Книга

Book [knýha]

Крокодил

Crocodile [krokodýl]

Квітка

Flower [kv'ítka]

Кіт

Cat [k'it]

Кк

Кільце

Ring [k'il'tsé]

Літак

Plane
[l'iták]

Лист

Letter [lyst]

Ложка

Spoon
[lózhka]

Лл

Ліс

Forrest
[l'is]

Лампа

Lamp
[lámpa]

Морозиво

Ice-cream
[morózyvo]

Машина

Car
[mashýna]

Мм

М'яч

Ball
[mjach]

Муха

Fly [múha]

Мапа

Map [mápa]

Намет

Tent [namét]

Ніс

Nose [n'is]

Нн

Ніж

Knife [n'izh]

Ноутбук

Laptop [noutbúk]

Нота

Note [nóta]

Олія

Oil
[ol'íja]

EXTRA VIRGIN

Окуляри

Glasses
[okul'áry]

Острів

Island
[óstr'iv]

Oo

Олень

Deer
[ólen']

Олівець

Pencil
[ol'ivéts']

Птах

Bird
[ptah]

Пес

Dog
[pes]

Пп

Пінгвін

Penguin
[p'inhv'ín]

Печиво

Cookies   [péchyvo]

Подарунок

Gift
[podarúnok]

Русалка

Mermaid
[rusálka]

Риба

Fish
[rýba]

Рp

Рюкзак

Backpack
[r'ukzák]

Рукавиця

Mitten
[rukavýts'a]

Рушник

Towel   [rushnýk]

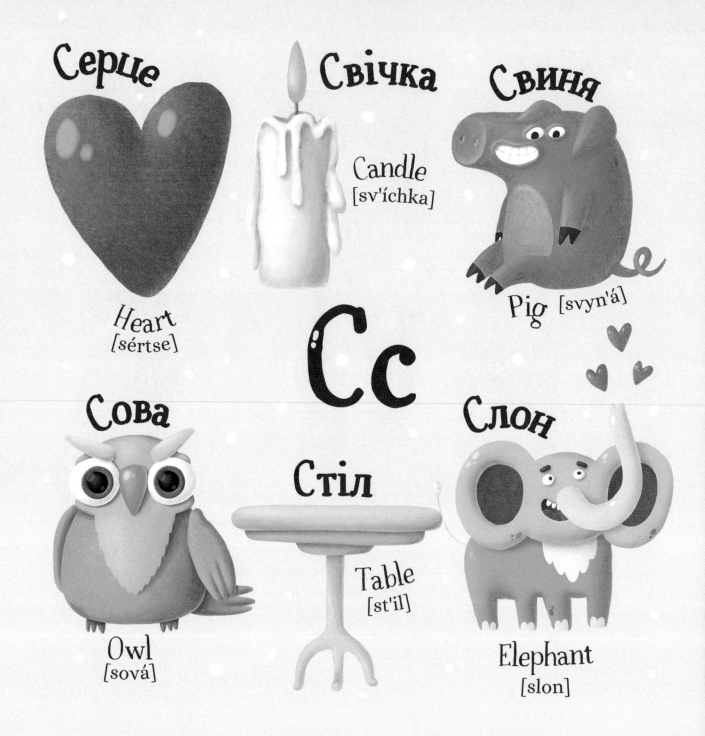

Серце
Heart
[sértse]

Свічка
Candle
[sv'íchka]

Свиня
Pig [svyn'á]

Cc

Сова
Owl
[sová]

Стіл
Table
[st'il]

Слон
Elephant
[slon]

Торт

Cake [tort]

Тюлень

Seal [t'ulén']

Т т

Телевізор

TV [telev'ízor]

Таксі

TAXI

Taxi [taks'í]

Трава

Grass [travá]

Україна

Ukraine
[ukrajína]

Учень

Pupil
[úchen']

Уу

Удав

Boa
[udáv]

Укол

Injection
[ukól]

Фотоапарат

Camera
[fotoaparát]

Фотографія

Photo
[fotohráfʹija]

Фф

Флaмінго

Flamingo
[flamʹínho]

Футболка

T-shirt
[futbólka]

Фісташка

Pistachio
[fistáshka]

Хліб

Bread
[hl'ib]

Хмара

Cloud
[hmára]

Xx

Хата

House
[háta]

Хот-дог

Hot dog   [hotdóg]

Цукерка

Candy

[tsukérka]

Цифра

123

Number [tsýfra]

Цц

Цуценя

Puppy

[tsutsen'á]

Цибуля

Onion

[tsybúl'a]

Черепаха

Turtle

[cherepáha]

Чипси

Chips [chýpsy]

Чч

Часник

Garlic [chasnýk]

Чайка

Gull

[chájka]

Човен

Boat [chóven]

Штани

Pants
[shtaný]

Шоколад

Chocolate
[shokolád]

Ш ш

Шпигун

Spy
[shpyhún]

Шкарпетка

Sock
[shkarpétka]

Шафа

Wardrobe
[sháfa]

Щур

Кущ

Щщ

Bush [kusch]

Rat [schur]

Дош

Щітка

Toothbrush [sch'itka]

Rain [dosch]

Бінокль

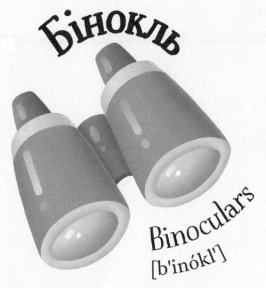

Binoculars
[b'inókl']

Ведмідь

Bear
[vedm'íd']

Ь

Soft
sign

Кінь

Horse
[k'in']

Корабель

Ship
[korabél']

Юнак

Young man
[junák]

Юнга

Cabin boy
[júnha]

Юю

Юпітер

Jupiter
[jup'íter]

Верблюд

Camel
[verbl'úd]

Якір

Anchor
[ják'ir]

Яблуко

Apple
[jábluko]

Яя

Ялинка

Яхта

Яйце

Yacht
[jáhta]

Egg
[jajtsé]

Fir-tree
[jalýnka]

Аа Бб Вв

Гг Гг Дд

Ее Єє Жж

Зз Ии Іі

Її Йй Кк

Лл Мм Нн

Оо Пп Рр

Сс Тт Уу

Фф Хх Цц

Чч Шш Щщ

ь Юю Яя

Made in United States
Troutdale, OR
09/12/2024

22763016R00024